What Do WASPs Say After Sex?

What Do WASPs Say After Sex?

Matt Freedman & Paul Hoffman

ST. MARTIN'S PRESS
NEW YORK

10 9 8 7 6 5 4 3 2 1
First Edition

Library of Congress Cataloging in Publication Data

Hoffman, Paul, 1956-
    What do WASPs say after sex?

    1. WASPs (Persons)—Anecdotes, facetiae,
satire, etc.   I. Freedman, Matt.   II. Title.
PN6231.W17H6   818'.5402   81-8902
ISBN 0-312-86585-6 (pbk.)   AACR2

Matt Freedman's photo by Charles Saltzman
Paul Hoffman's photo by Philip Tugendrajch

To Amy Vanderbilt

What Do WASPs Say After Sex?

WASP / wäsp, wȯsp / n. (*White Anglo-Saxon Protestant*): an American of Northern European and esp. British stock and of Protestant background: one often considered to be a member of the dominating and most privileged class of people in the U.S.

How can you tell the WASPs in a Chinese restaurant?

They're the ones not sharing the food.

How do you tell if a WASP is sexually excited?

He has a stiff upper lip.

What do you get when you cross a WASP and a gorilla?

An athletic scholarship to Harvard.

What do you get when you cross a WASP and a Jew?

Pushy Pilgrims.

What's a WASP's idea of post-coital depression?

Not being able to reach *The New Yorker* from the bed.

What do WASPS think public transportation is?

The Martha's Vineyard ferry.

How do you drive a WASP insane?

Invite him to roll a few frames at the Yale Bowl.

Why did God create WASPs?

(Somebody had to buy retail.)

What do WASPs think Zimbabwe Rhodesia is?

(A wide receiver for the Houston Oilers.)

Boat People

MY FATHER GRADUATED FROM EXETER.
MY GRANDFATHER GRADUATED FROM EXETER
MY GREAT GRANDFATHER GRADUATED FROM
EXETER. EVERYBODY IN MY
FAMILY GRADUATED FROM EXETER

MY GREAT GREAT GREAT
GRANDMOTHER CAME ACROSS
WITH MILES STANDISH. MY
GREAT GREAT
GREAT UNCLE
WON THE CIVIL
WAR. MY FAM...

MY GREAT GREAT, GREAT, GREAT, GREAT, GREAT GRAND AUNT WAS QUEEN ELIZABETH! MY GREAT, GREAT, GREAT, GREAT COUSIN WAS St GEORGE!

MY FAMILY FOUGHT WITH ALEXANDER THE GREAT. MY FAMILY WAS EATEN BY LIONS IN THE COLISEUM. MY FAM

19

WE HAD OUR
OWN BOAT.

21

How do you deflower a WASP?

Buy her a western saddle.

How do WASPs find the toilet in the dark?

They feel around for the fuzziest chair in the house.

Why do WASPs swim only on their backs?

They don't like to get their Topsiders wet.

How do you make a WASP cat happy?

Mate it with a cashmere sweater.

How do WASP doggies bark?

They don't, they sniff.

What do WASPs think of the labor
movement?

(Caesarians are much less embarrassing.)

How does a WASP know it's involved in
a long-term sexual relationship?

(It experiences increasing guilt and
mounting disrespect for its partner.)

What do you get when you cross a WASP and an orangutan?

I don't know. But whatever it is, it won't let you in its cage.

What do WASPs say when they make love?

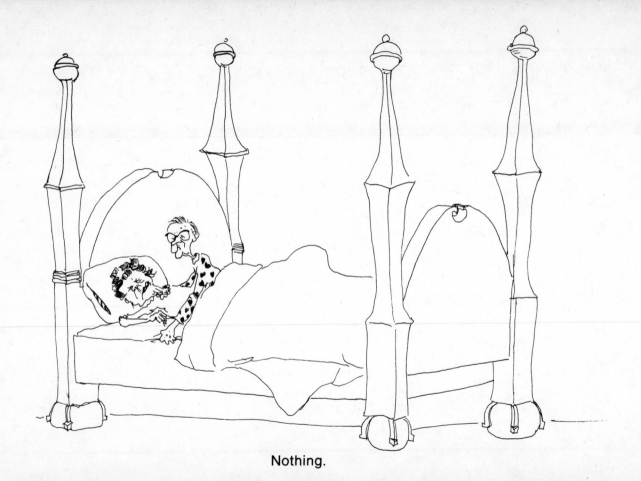

Nothing.

What do you get when you cross a WASP
and a Puerto Rican?

Assault and battery.

A Cautionary Tail

What's a WASP's idea of open-mindedness?

Dating a Canadian.

What do WASPs say
after sex?

"Thank you very much. I'm sorry. It won't happen again."

What does a little WASP boy
want to be when he grows up?

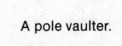

A pole vaulter.

What does a little WASP girl
want to be when she grows up?

"The very best person I possibly can."

How do you tell when a preppy
is in mourning?

His collar is at half mast.

Mrs. Fairchild and her son Twig were relaxing at the beach in Bar Harbor. Twig took a dip too soon after cocktails. He started to sink. The lifeguard dived into the water, pulled Twig to the surface and dragged him to shore. "We'll have to use artificial respiration."

"No!" shrieked Mrs. Fairchild. "The real thing or nothing at all!"

45

A Sunfish with a spinnaker.

What's a WASP's idea of social security?

(An ancestor on the Mayflower.)

Who is the WASP's favorite actor of all time?

(Rin Tin Tin.)

49

What would happen if a UFO
landed in a WASP's backyard?

That all depends...

How does a WASP know when his wife
is prepared to have sex?

(She comes to bed wearing only gloves.)

What do you get when you cross a WASP
and a Black?

(A conversation piece.)

What's a WASP occupational hazard?

Rope burns from the ski lift.

How do you tell the WASP woman at
a nudist colony?

She's the one wearing the wire
brassiere.

53

Red, White, Blue and Black

Why did the WASP cross the street?

To get to the middle of the road.

Why do WASPs send their kids to prep school?

Preparatory school offers challenging academic opportunities that expand the mind, compulsory afternoon sports that build character and a stimulating social environment that encourages individual growth at the same time that it promotes group identity.

How can you tell when a Groton
graduate is a failure?

The Alumni Office seats him in the end
zone at Homecoming.

How do you tell a WASP teenager?

His alligator has acne.

How can you tell a WASP baby girl?

She has a diaper wrapped around her shoulders.

What happens when four WASPs find
themselves in the same room?

A dinner party.

Why do so many WASPs go into high finance?

Stocks and bonds are in their blood.

How do WASPs wean their young?

They fire the maid.

What do WASPs think of the Mideast situation?

(Well, Newport is all right, but *everybody* goes to the Cape.)

What do WASPs do with their old people?

(They put them in Jeep Scout Masters and drive them off cliffs in New Canaan.)

A Cross to Bear

What's a preppy headmistress's idea of suicide?

Second degree murder.

How does a WASP propose marriage?

He asks, "How would you like to be buried with my people?"   75

What's the best way to confuse a WASP?

Invite him to Passover Seder
and sing Harvard fight songs.

What's a WASP's idea of affirmative
action?

Hiring South American jockeys.

How do you tell the bride at a WASP wedding?

She's the one kissing the golden retriever.

How do WASPs know when it's raining?

Water gets in their noses.